PELARGONIUMS

AN ILLUSTRATED GUIDE TO VARIETIES, CULTIVATION AND CARE, WITH STEP-BY-STEP INSTRUCTIONS AND OVER 170 BEAUTIFUL PHOTOGRAPHS

Blaise Cooke

Consultant: Hazel Key
Photography by Marie O'Hara

southwater

This edition is published by Southwater
an imprint of Anness Publishing Ltd
info@anness.com
www.southwaterbooks.com
www.annesspublishing.com

If you like the images in this book and would like to investigate
using them for publishing, promotions or advertising, please visit
our website www.practicalpictures.com for more information.

A CIP catalogue record for this book is available from the British Library.

Publisher: Joanna Lorenz
Senior Editor: Cathy Marriott
Designer: Michael Morey
Production Controller: Ben Worley

PUBLISHER'S NOTE
Although the advice and information in this book are believed to be accurate and true at the time
of going to press, neither the authors nor the publisher can accept any legal responsibility or liability
for any errors or omissions that may have been made nor for any inaccuracies nor for any loss,
harm or injury that comes about from following instructions or advice in this book.

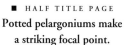

■ HALF TITLE PAGE
**Potted pelargoniums make
a striking focal point.**
■ FRONTISPIECE
P. 'Ashley Stephenson'
■ TITLE PAGE
P. 'Fleur d'Amour'

■ LEFT
A mixed planting arrangement.
■ OPPOSITE LEFT
P. 'Margaret Waite'
■ OPPOSITE RIGHT
P. cucullatum

PELARGONIUMS

Contents

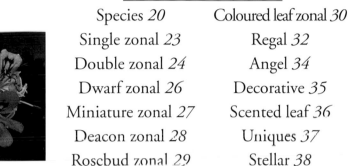

Introduction

*F*ew other groups of garden plants are as widely grown, or contribute as much colour to summer planting displays, as pelargoniums. They are grown for the visual impact of their flowers, for their coloured foliage, or for the rich aromatic oils which are released from warm or bruised leaves. Introduced to cultivation in the seventeenth century, the group is now popular throughout the world.

The botanical name *Pelargonium* refers to the shape of the fruit or seed head. Just before it is ripe, the fruit appears sharply beaked, and is reminiscent of a stork, or *pelargos* in Greek.

This book will lead you through the simple techniques involved in growing and propagating these plants, and illustrates some of the most popular cultivars available.

■ RIGHT
The vibrant colour from pelargoniums will lift and enliven every garden scene.

The history of pelargoniums

The introduction of pelargoniums to the gardens and conservatories of Europe is closely linked to the exploration of the globe and, in particular, the southern seas. Wild *Pelargonium* species almost all originate in the warm-temperate or subtropical regions of South Africa. They grow in dry, frost-free conditions in southern Africa, and a few are native to Australia.

Throughout the sixteenth, seventeenth and eighteenth centuries, the European colonial powers imported a great many wild plants, including many *Pelargonium* species. Arriving first in Holland with ships of the Dutch East India Company and later coming directly to Britain from the Cape, which was then a British colony, these plants were grown across Europe in botanic gardens,

in specialist nurseries and in the gardens of plant enthusiasts. Plants moved quickly between the countries of Europe. *P. peltatum*, for example, was introduced to Holland in 1700, and the species is known to have been grown in Britain by the Duchess of Beaufort in Chelsea only a year later.

There are several early records of *Pelargonium* cultivation, amongst which, in a revised edition of

■ LEFT
Pots and containers are ideal for pelargoniums, and grouped together they make a wonderful focal point in a garden.

**Golden variegated leaves will brighten
a sombre corner.**

Gerard's *Herbal* produced in 1633,
there is a description of a tuberous-
rooted plant grown by John
Tradescant of Lambeth, London.
The plant was named *Geranium
Indicum Noctu Odoratum*, and from
the description it was most probably
the night-scented *Pelargonium triste*.
This species became well known in
Europe, as it was frequently collected
by sailors returning from the east, and
the tuber was used in herbal remedies
for the treatment of dysentery.

Pelargonium species with scented
leaves soon became popular as pot
plants, and it did not take long for
particular named varieties to arise
from hybridization of these species
plants. *Pelargonium* 'Lady Plymouth',
for example, was supposedly
a silver sport of the species
P. capitatum; it was later thought
the species was *P. graveolens*, but
recent examination of the *graveolens*
plants shows it is not a true species
but a hybrid, and is therefore called
P. 'Graveolens' Hort.

Many of the new species arriving
in Europe from different parts of
Africa at that time were grown
together, almost side by side, in the
gardens and stove houses (heated
greenhouses) of collectors. Species
in which flowering was separated in

nature by distance or season were no
longer separated. This had a great
impact on the development of the
Pelargonium hybrids as spontaneous
hybridization could take place, with
the help of bees, amongst plants that
would not normally grow together in
the wild. *Pelargonium inquinans*, and
P. zonale, for example, both of which
are important as the parents of the
'Zonal' pelargoniums, were
introduced into cultivation in

Europe in the seventeenth century,
though significant advances in the
development of 'Zonal' pelargoniums
did not take place until the early
nineteenth century. Most efforts
seemed to be concentrated on what
were to become the 'Regal' and
'Unique' pelargoniums.

The popularity of pelargoniums
has been cyclic; fashions and the
focus of interest have varied with
time. There was a peak of interest in

The full, pink heads of this pelargonium increase the sense of heat from the orange lilies behind.

the early nineteenth century due perhaps to improvements in the glass industry and the identification of new cultivars. For example, 'Lady Scarborough', a variety of *P. crispum*, was identified in the early 1800s, and became popular for its sweet, lemon-scented leaves. The dominant species then was *P. cucullatum* and its subspecies. Larger-flowered groups, such as the 'Regals' and the 'Uniques', were gaining popularity.

Increasingly, through the Victorian era, 'Regal' pelargoniums became very popular in both Britain and America. This was probably in response to the interest in them expressed by the British royal family and the leading American families. The cultivars grown during this time were tall plants. 'Lord Bute', at 45cm (18in), was considered normal, but today this would be considered tall. Only a few varieties from this era are still widely grown, having been surpassed by the modern cultivars which are shorter, and produce flowers over a longer period.

From about 1820 onwards, some cultivars were raised from a plant called 'Angelique'. 'Angel' pelargoniums are shrubby with small leaves, below miniature, 'Regal'-like flowers. An enthusiast called Mr Langley Smith undertook to develop the true 'Angel' group in the early 1930s, using *P. crispum* as one of the parents. It has been suggested that the Langley Smith hybrids are similar to the 'Angelique' cultivars, and that they should all be grouped under one name, 'Angels'. However, the so-called 'Angeliques' do not have *P. crispum*, or a form of it, in their parentage, as all true 'Angels' do, and have now been assigned to the 'Decorative' group.

From Mr Langley Smith's work many notable varieties arose, such as 'Catford Belle' and several others which are still popular today.

The history and development of pelargoniums in cultivation have been enriched by the efforts of enthusiastic amateur and specialist growers around the world who developed a specialism in hybridizing a unique line of cultivars. Particularly amongst the 'Zonal' pelargoniums, several subgroups of plants exist that are named after the grower or after one of the parent cultivars. The group

■ LEFT
This robust pelargonium has been allowed to grow into a full and striking specimen.

known as 'Irenes', for example, arose from the cultivar 'Irene', introduced in America in 1942 by Charles Behringer of Ohio. Later 'Irene' types were produced during the 1950s, the result of crosses using 'Irene' as one parent. These plants are still very popular today, especially in Britain. The 'Zonal' pelargoniums known as 'Deacons' were also the result of work carried out by an enthusiast, Canon

Stringer, who worked on the selective breeding between a miniature 'Zonal' and an 'Ivy-leaved' pelargonium in the 1970s.

During recent years there has been a great interest in the production of dwarf and miniature plants suitable for growing on narrow windowsills and for use in small gardens. One such plant is 'Wendy Read', a natural dwarf double raised in 1974.

■ RIGHT
Use a cluster of flower-filled pots to enhance a garden feature.

Pelargoniums in conservatory and garden

Pelargoniums are a wonderfully varied group of plants which lend themselves perfectly to cultivation in pots, containers and as seasonal bedding in the garden or even the herb garden. From a broad and diverse group of species, a remarkable number of cultivars has been produced, providing a rich choice of plants for any position in the conservatory or garden.

In the conservatory

Pelargoniums are ideally suited to cultivation in greenhouses or conservatories, where a good light, an even temperature and airy conditions will encourage strong and healthy growth. Pelargonium cultivars with scented leaves are amongst the traditional plants grown in conservatories, and will thrive where some direct light will warm their leaves. This encourages the release of their aromatic oils, which make a wonderful natural air-freshener. Most of the scented-leaved plants will grow rapidly, so regular trimming or pruning is necessary to keep them in shape.

Any of the 'Regal' pelargoniums, with their large and often frilled flowers, will make a striking display in a conservatory. Modern 'Regal' cultivars, which are repeat flowering

CONSERVATORY
'Apple Blossom Rosebud'
'Ashfield Jubilee'
'Ashley Stephenson'
'Bird Dancer'
'Deacon Mandarin'
'Lady Plymouth'
'Lady Scarborough'
'Moon Maiden'
'Mr Henry Cox'
'Occold Shield'
'Patricia Andrea'

and produce blooms throughout the summer, grow into an attractive, leafy dome above which the glorious mass of flowers is arrayed. These plants can be presented as specimens, grown in a decorative or clay pot, or as a harmoniously arranged group.

The bright, strong colours of the 'Zonal' cultivars will enliven and enrich a conservatory, whether grown for variegated and decorative foliage, or as specimen flowering plants grown alone or amongst a group of foliage plants. Most of the 'Zonal' cultivars will produce flowers throughout the summer, and will even flower during the winter months if grown in a sufficiently bright and warm position. Older plants can grow up to 2–3m (6–10ft) tall, but the stems may become bare as they grow woody, preventing young shoots breaking from low down. Regular cutting back will encourage fresh growth.

Indoor or windowsill cultivation

Miniature pelargoniums are perfect for indoor and windowsill cultivation where space is limited. They will bloom for months and even throughout the year on a sunny windowsill. Most true miniatures grow to not more than 13cm (5in) tall, and can be maintained in 9cm (3.5in) pots.

Compact 'Ivy-leaved' pelargoniums, such as 'Golden Lilac Gem', grown as tumbling plants or tied up against a flat, decorative pot trellis, can be attractive, adding height to a windowsill collection. 'Angel' pelargoniums are amongst the most suitable for windowsill cultivation. They tend to be small and compact, and their leaves are often delicately scented – a result of *Pelargonium crispum* in their parentage.

Mature 'Regal' pelargonium plants are suited to growing as house plants, but because they often grow to 45cm (18in) tall, they may be considered too large when fully grown for most indoor situations.

WINDOWSILLS

'Bird Dancer'

'Deacon Mandarin'

'Lady Scarborough'

'Little Gem'

PAC 'Lovesong'

'Mr Everaarts'

'Occold Shield'

'Old Spice'

'Wallis Friesdorf'

'Wendy Read'

they often have pleasantly scented foliage, and their strong, tall growth makes an attractive foil to other plants, grown at their base.

As bedding plants

Pelargoniums are prime plants for use in summer bedding schemes; tolerant of dry conditions, plants will flower well throughout the warm months. Seed-grown F1 hybrid 'Zonal' single cultivars, such as 'Freckles', are often used for bedding because they will give a uniform performance. Semi-double and double-flowered cultivars are particularly suitable for bedding, because of their splendidly large flower heads. If there is a long wet spell, though, these blooms can hold the

As container plants

Containers such as window boxes, patio tubs and pots or hanging baskets, planted with a single pelargonium cultivar or with a mixed group of plants, can add a bright, highly decorative dimension to any warm, outdoor position. Dwarf cultivars are particularly suited to window boxes where the height of the plants may be important and where root growth may be restricted. Mix dwarf 'Zonal' cultivars with some 'Ivy-leaved' plants

so that you develop a falling tapestry of colour. 'Ivy-leaved' plants will produce a wonderful display throughout the summer, and well into the early months of autumn, especially if they are mature plants in their second summer of growth. 'Scented leaf' pelargoniums are old favourites for window boxes, and their refreshing aroma coming through an open window will fill the room on a warm day. Cultivars from the 'Unique' group of pelargoniums are striking grown in patio pots, as

IN A FLOWER BORDER

'Ashfield Jubilee'
'Crimson Unique'
'Irene'
'Lord Bute'
'Mr Henry Cox'
'Mrs Pollock'
'Pink Aurore's Unique'
'Royal Ascot'
'Sancho Panza'
'Scarlet Rambler'

Pelargoniums are ideal as summer bedding plants as they flower well throughout the warm months.

Create a lovely festive atmosphere by gathering some flowering pots around your garden table.

In the garden

In frost-prone regions, plants can be grown in containers or as summer bedding and lifted to a frost-free location for over-wintering. In frost-free regions, pelargoniums can be grown as an addition to any sunny flower border. Dwarf, miniature or

'Scented leaf' cultivars can be used as edging plants for the border or along a pathway. Taller 'Unique' or 'Decorative' varieties grown towards the back of the border will give height to the planting. Rich-flowered 'Regal' and 'Angel' pelargoniums planted in a border will bring an intensity of colour and texture to the scheme.

rainwater, which means they will have to be dead-headed. As a general rule, a more striking impact will be achieved if blocks of only one or two cultivars are planted together, rather than mixing several cultivars in one scheme.

Ornamental-leaved plants such as *P.* 'Happy Thought', which has striking pale cream or yellow-green, edged leaves, each with a pale brown central zone, and small, single, crimson flowers, can provide extra interest to a planting.

A 'Zonal' cultivar, single- or double-flowered, grown as a standard or semi-standard specimen, will create a focal point and raise the height of the bedding scheme. Cultivars grown as standard plants, which have a contrasting flower and leaf colour to the main low-level planting, will add vibrancy. Dwarf cultivars can be used as edging plants, and even the 'Ivy-leaved' cultivars are useful as bedding – their stems act as a weed-suppressing ground cover, and their shiny, stiff leaves withstand the rain.

Botanical classification of pelargoniums

A mixed bunch of garden and conservatory plants are commonly but incorrectly called 'geraniums'. The name is often used to cover two different but related groups of plants: pelargoniums and geraniums. To add to the confusion, the general names, pelargonium and geranium, mimic the scientific names, *Pelargonium* and *Geranium*, which are differentiated only by the use of italics and capital letters.

The botanical group, or genus *Geranium*, is widespread throughout the temperate regions. These plants are usually frost-hardy and are commonly grown in gardens throughout the temperate world. In contrast, the natural distribution of the genus *Pelargonium*, with its 230 species, is almost entirely confined to the southern warm-temperate or sub-tropical areas. The plants are almost all frost-tender, and are grown for summer colour in gardens, and in conservatories as pot plants.

The plants united within the genus *Pelargonium* are very diverse, but the species have several characteristics in common, particularly those of the flowers. These characteristics are also those that separate them from their sister genus *Geranium*. *Pelargonium* flowers are always irregular in shape, some species have five petals, others appear to have only two or four. All *Pelargonium* flowers have two large upper petals, and up to three smaller lower petals. In the centre of the flower are the pollen-bearing stamens, of which there are ten. *Pelargonium* species have up to seven of the ten fertile stamens. *Geraniums*, however, have regular, symmetrical flowers which carry ten fertile stamens.

Scientific examination has led to the determination of what appear to be, at present, sixteen distinct, natural groups or sections within the single *Pelargonium* genus. These sections are united by features such as plant habit, leaf character, the presence of aromatic oils and glandular hairs, the structure of the flower heads as well as, more simply, the geographical distribution of the species. The section Pelargonium itself, for example, unites several species, such

■ RIGHT
Single flowers are often large and well spaced.

■ LEFT
The flowers of 'Rosebud' cultivars are tightly clustered.

■ RIGHT
The flowers of tulip varieties resemble miniature tulips.

Species flowers are usually simple and primitive in appearance. This flower shows the two upper large petals, each marked with a large purple blotch, and three, smaller lower petals. The stamens can be seen grouped in the centre.

as *P. capitatum* and *P. crispum*, which are economically important for the extraction of valuable essential oils. The section Polyactium, unites *P. fulgidum* and *P. triste*, on the basis that they all have five-petalled, star-like, night-scented flowers, and tuberous roots. Many of the species which are important as parents of the modern cultivars, such as *P. inquinans* and *P. zonale*, are grouped within the section Ciconium and originate from the Cape Province, from where they were early introductions to Europe.

Most pelargoniums grow as evergreen perennials in regions which are dry and frost-free. Their stems and leaves are often succulent or slightly succulent as a result of adaptation to these dry habitats. *P. peltatum*, for example, has thick, waxy leaves which resist water loss. *P. triste* has developed an under ground resistance: its roots have become swollen as storage organs into thick tuber-like structures.

There is such a wealth of leaf shapes, textures and even leaf colours exhibited by the various wild *Pelargonium* species that they often appear to be from totally different families. Large round leaves are produced by *P. inquinans*; *P. peltatum* has thick, almost waxy fleshy leaves; *P. triste* has feathery, carrot-like leaves, and the leaves of *P. fulgidum* are soft and silky. *P. zonale*, the parent of the 'Zonal' pelargoniums, introduces the dark, zonal band which identifies many plants in this group.

Plant growth is slow in dry conditions, so several species have developed protection against browsing animals or leaf eating

■ LEFT
Double flowers.

■ LEFT
A 'Stellar' variety flower head.

■ LEFT
Cactus varieties have rolled petals.

■ BELOW

The green centre of this tri-coloured leaf is surrounded by an almost white margin, overlaid with a red zonal band.

■ BELOW

This tri-colour leaf has a rich cream outer margin.

■ BELOW

'Zonal' geraniums can have almost plain green leaves, with only a faint band.

insects by developing strongly scented and aromatic leaves which may act as a deterrent. The aromatic leaf scents can be heritable, and may give a clue to the parentage of some of the cultivars. The pungent smell of 'Zonal' pelargoniums is widely recognized and has probably been inherited from the parent species *P. inquinans*. Some of the aromatic oils released from the foliage of other pelargoniums can be highly attractive. The citrus-scented leaves carried by some of the 'Angel' cultivars are an indication of *P. crispum* in their parentage.

For amateur growers, the genus *Pelargonium* has been artificially divided into several groups which unite the man-made varieties of cultivated pelargoniums that have similar characteristics. 'Zonal', 'Regal', 'Angel', 'Decorative', 'Ivy-leaved' and 'Unique' pelargoniums are the major artificial groups, within which there are further divisions.

'Zonal' pelargoniums

Considered to be the 'basic geranium', these cultivars are usually covered with blooms and bring a bright splash of colour to any situation. Botanically, the section is known as *P.* × *hortorum*, and it is likely that several species played a role in its parentage, amongst which were *P. zonale* and *P. inquinans*, both of which have red flowers.

The leaves can be either mainly green or with a pale yellow/cream variegation, and most carry a dark band which can be striking or less visible. These are the popular and widely grown plants which produce brilliant displays of colour in bedding schemes, patio and conservatory pots, on windowsills and in window boxes.

'Zonal' pelargoniums are further divided into:
■ Single-flowered plants which embrace most of the modern seed-raised cultivars

■ Semi-double and double-flowered plants which have large, full flowers
■ Dwarf 'Zonals' which can be single- or double-flowered and have arisen in cultivation from 'Zonal' varieties
■ Miniature 'Zonals' which are either single- or double-flowered and which became popular in the 1950s
■ Deacon 'Zonals' which were bred by Canon Stringer to be dwarf, double and compact cultivars
■ Rosebud-flowered plants which are double flowered, with many broad, rolled petals
■ Coloured foliage 'Zonals' which can have bi- or tri-coloured leaves

'Regal' pelargoniums

Officially known as *P.* × *domesticum*, (or otherwise as 'Martha Washington', and 'Lady Washington', 'show pelargoniums' or 'grandiflorums'), this group is derived from crosses between *P. angulosum*, *P. cucullatum*, *P. fulgidum*, and *P. grandiflorum*.

'Stellar' cultivars have maple-shaped leaves;
here the leaf is dark brown, with a narrow,
golden-green margin.

■ ABOVE
'Ivy-leaved' pelargoniums have a glossy,
almost waxy texture.

'Angel' pelargoniums

These decorative plants were derived
from a 'Regal' pelargonium, 'The
Shah', and *P. crispum*; they became
popular in the 1900s. This group is
no longer classed as miniature 'Regals'
but accepted as a separate group.

'Decorative' pelargoniums

Often listed in directories under
the 'Regal' or 'Angel' sections,
these old-fashioned 'Regals' differ
from the modern varieties by virtue
of the small size of their leaves
and flowers.

'Scented leaf' pelargoniums

These perennials are grown for
their leaves, which release scent
when brushed or warmed. The
cultivated plants are still allied to
the pure species plants from which
they have arisen, and bear small,
simple flowers.

'Unique' pelargoniums

These are usually large, shrubby
plants which have aromatic leaves
and flowers borne on short stems.
P. fulgidum is generally considered to
be the main, and possibly the female
parent of this group, together with
P. cucullatum which may have been
responsible for the mauve colouration
in the flowers and for the scent, shape
and softness of the foliage.

■ RIGHT
The small,
scented leaves of
this cultivar are
strongly aromatic
when warmed or
bruised.

'Stellar' pelargoniums

These were derived from crosses
between *P. staphysagroides* and
P. × hortorum. The flowers are
irregularly star-shaped, either single
or double, and the leaves are markedly
star-shaped with pointed lobes.

'Ivy-leaved' pelargoniums

Often known as 'basket' or 'trailing'
pelargoniums, this group was
developed approximately 300 years
ago from *P. peltatum,* from which
come the shield-like leaves held
centrally on their leaf stalk or petiole.

Species *Pelargonium*

Plant Directory

In the following plant directory, pelargoniums are arranged in the different artificial groups which unite the man-made varieties of cultivated plants. These groups have been devised for amateur gardeners and have no botanical significance. The dimensions given are those which the plants will attain under normal conditions. Each cultivar is accompanied by a recommendation on its suitability for use in pots, containers, window boxes or as garden plants. Planted with due consideration of local climatic conditions, they make a wonderful addition to any indoor or outside planting arrangement.

■ RIGHT
PELARGONIUM ZONALE

This species is to be found wild, scrambling through supporting bushes and other vegetation, in the eastern and western Cape Province. A robust plant whose stems can grow to 1m (40in) long. The leaves are round, usually with a dark, horseshoe marking or zonal band. The flowers are most often pink, rarely white or red, borne in clusters on long flower stalks and lifted well above the foliage. One of the parents of the 'Zonal' group of pelargoniums.

Many of the *Pelargonium* species grow into much bigger plants than their cultivated varieties, often with a shrubby or scrambling form. The flowers are usually small, simple and classed as primitive. The species described here have all played an important role in the development of the major decorative groups of pelargonium.

PELARGONIUM CUCULLATUM

The name 'cucullatum' means cup-like and refers to the leaf form, which can be cupped. Plants grow as big shrubs and carry large flowers united in few-flowered heads. The flowers are bright purple-pink, and can have a diameter of up to 4cm (1½in). This plant originates from the Cape Province, but there seem to be several sub-species which occur in isolated locations. The flower size and leaf texture indicate that this species has played a role in the parentage of the 'Unique' and 'Regal' pelargonium groups.

■ ABOVE

PELARGONIUM INQUINANS

An erect, self-branching plant which can grow to over 2m (6ft) tall. The stems are covered with small, red glandular hairs which will leave a stain on hands and fingers. The leaves are soft and almost circular in shape. The flowers are scarlet, occasionally pink or white, and are carried in heads of up to 20 in total. This species, together with *P. zonale*, has played an important role as one of the original parents in the production of the 'Zonal' group.

■ RIGHT

PELARGONIUM FRUTETORUM

A spreading, self-branching plant which has thick, red-brown stems and which grows to form a shrub. The leaves have rounded lobes and carry a dark zonal band inside the margin; the flowers arc pale salmon-pink. A useful species which can tolerate shade. It has been used in hybridizing programmes to produce 'Zonal' plants which have decorative foliage, such as those with bi- and tri-coloured leaves.

■ BELOW

PELARGONIUM BETULINUM

Named because the shape of its leaves resembles birch leaves, this species occurs wild along the south-western and southern coasts of South Africa. It grows in the same region as *P. cucullatum,* and it is likely that the two hybridize naturally in the wild. The flowers are large, pink or purple-pink, less commonly white, the upper petals heavily veined with purple-red, all arranged in clusters of three to four flowers. This is a very decorative plant, and is important as it is almost certainly one of the parents of the 'Regal' and 'Unique' pelargoniums.

■ BELOW

PELARGONIUM FULGIDUM

Not usually considered to be a highly attractive plant, this species is semi-succulent, deciduous, and carries deeply lobed leaves on leggy stems which can grow to almost 50cm (20in) tall. The flowers are bright red, a feature which is passed to offspring when this species is used as the pollen-donating plant in a hybridization. 'Regal' pelargoniums have inherited their flower colour from this species.

■ LEFT

PELARGONIUM TRISTE

Named 'sad' because of the dull flower colour, this was perhaps the first species pelargonium introduced to cultivation in Europe. Plants form large, fleshy tubers from which short, succulent stems arise bearing deeply divided, carrot-like hairy leaves. The flowers can be brownish-purple or sometimes yellow or brown, and are remarkably strongly night-scented. A delightful little plant to grow, not only for its decorative leaves but mostly for the striking flower scent which is released nightly.

Single zonal pelargoniums

Considered to be the 'basic geranium', these simple-flowered cultivars are usually covered with blooms. Although easily grown from cuttings and not from seed, most of the modern seed-raised cultivars belong to this group.

■ ABOVE
'BLISS'

A large-flowered cultivar with attractive, pale coral-pink flowers which have a clear, white centre. Plants can attain 35cm (14in) in height, and are highly suitable for growing as bedding, or in a window box or terrace planter.

■ LEFT
'JOAN FONTAINE'

A reliable cultivar which has dark green leaves below pale salmon-pink flowers each lit by a small, white eye. Plants are self-branching and bushy, growing to approximately 25–30cm (10–12in) tall. A wonderful bedding plant, the leaves and the flowers are quite weather resistant.

■ LEFT
'MILLFIELD RIVAL'

A modern cultivar which is robust and short-jointed, forming bushy plants up to 25cm (10in) tall. The flowers are soft, rose-pink with a white eye. This is a strong plant which can be grown as a standard to create an impact in a summer planting.

Double zonal pelargoniums

These are the popular and widely grown plants which produce brilliant displays of colour in bedding schemes, patio and conservatory pots, on windowsills and in window boxes. They are best grown as biennials, and usually benefit from pinching out of the growing points to encourage branching. Double flowers are those which each have eight or more petals; semi-double flowers have between five and eight petals. The mass of petals often replaces pollen- and seed-forming parts of the flower and so double flowers rarely attract insects or set seeds.

■ OPPOSITE
TOP LEFT
'ROSE IRENE'

A commendable variety which, like the others in the 'Irene' section, will grow well through the winter from autumn cuttings. The flowers are produced in large heads, and are rose-pink with a white eye. Ideal for growing as part of a mixed summer display in tubs or pots.

■ ABOVE
'SPRINGTIME'

Introduced in America in 1942, by Charles Behringer of Ohio, this 'Irene' cultivar produces semi-double, salmon-coral flowers over a long period. Plants are short-jointed and so bushier than most 'Irenes' and will only attain 40cm (16in) in height. They are very reliable for use as bedding plants.

■ LEFT
'IRENE'

Introduced in America in 1942, by Charles Behringer, this is one of the parents of the sub-section known as the 'Irene' cultivars. Later 'Irene' types were produced during the 1950s and were very popular but are less so today because they tend to grow to almost 45cm (18in) tall. 'Irene' carries large crimson, semi-double flowers which are produced continuously in generous clusters almost 11cm (4.5in) in diameter, whilst the plants are warm and well lit. Invaluable in a flower border where its flowers and its size make a strong impact.

■ ABOVE MIDDLE
PELFI 'BLUES'

'Pelfi' is the prefix used to identify pelargoniums raised and
marketed by Fischer from Germany, and is an indication of plants
which are compact, self-branching and whose foliage and flowers
exhibit maximum weather resistance. Distribution of these cultivars
is through selected nurseries. The flowers of 'Blues' are pink, large
and semi-double. The plants will attain 25–30cm (10–12in) in
height and are highly suitable for growing in window boxes and
as centre-pieces in hanging baskets.

■ ABOVE RIGHT
PAC 'LOVESONG'

PAC is the trade mark of Wilhelm Elsner of Dresden; several of
these plants, such as 'Lovesong', are bound under Plant Breeders'
Rights, and so may only be propagated under licence. A remarkable
cultivar which carries lovely pink flowers, marked with a red dot
on each petal. Plants will grow to almost 30cm (12in) tall, and
are striking grown as part of a mixed planting or in a window box.

■ RIGHT
PELFI 'SCHÖNE HELENA'

Easy to grow, these robust, erect plants are short-jointed and form a
stocky, compact, dense bush up to 40cm (16in) tall, with attractively
zoned leaves. The flowers are semi-double, large, clear salmon in
colour and are produced in large flower heads freely throughout the
summer. Ideal for bedding or use in a mixed planting.

Dwarf zonal pelargoniums

Dwarf 'Zonal' pelargoniums are the answer to all the space restrictions imposed by modern buildings. These plants only grow to 13–20cm (5–8in) in height and are usually delightfully floriferous. They are normally grown in 9cm (3.5in) pots and are self-branching and bushy.

■ LEFT
'OCCOLD SHIELD'

From the stable of Canon Stringer who bred the 'Deacon' cultivars, this plant has green-gold leaves, each emblazoned with a dark, central shield-shaped zone. The flowers are single, orangey-pink and arranged in fairly dense heads. Plants will probably grow slightly taller than 20cm (8in) but are still commendable for use on windowsills or as the centre planting in a hanging basket, or in tubs, pots or window boxes.

■ ABOVE
'WALLIS FRIESDORF'

A glorious little plant which has stately dark, almost black, leaves below deep-rose to scarlet, semi-double flowers which have narrow petals. This is one of the oldest dwarf cultivars in cultivation, known since 1927. Often listed in directories as 'Friesdorf', it is an impressive plant for window boxes or garden tubs.

■ ABOVE
'MR EVERAARTS'

A modern American variety which grows as a neat, bushy plant and carries its rose-pink double flowers well above the soft green leaves. Self-branching, the plants grow to less than 20cm (8in) tall and are ideal for window boxes.

Miniature zonal pelargoniums

Extremely popular but often scarce in nurseries, miniature 'Zonals' are ideal for narrow windowsills and small conservatories. Flowers are produced over a long period, and both single- and double-flowered cultivars are available. The leaves are often dark green. Miniatures should be no taller than 13cm (5in).

■ ABOVE
'SILVER KEWENSE'

A stunning little plant which has the bonus of variegated silver and green leaves. The flowers are single, crimson and appear fairly primitive with narrow petals. Several of these plants grouped together in any container will make a truly striking display.

■ ABOVE
'RED BLACK VESUVIUS'

Considered to be one of the oldest miniature varieties, this cultivar was produced in 1890. Plants are not robust, and grow well within the 13cm (5in) height which typifies this group. The flowers are single, rich scarlet, and produced abundantly above the almost black leaves, which are each marked with an even darker zonal band. Best suited to windowsill locations where the light is very bright.

■ BELOW
'KESGRAVE'

A modern cultivar which was raised in 1983. The flowers are double, orange-pink and very attractive above the dark leaves. The slightly muted colour makes them suitable as a summer infill on a rockery but they are best grown as a pot plant.

Deacon zonal pelargoniums

'Deacons' are the result of selective breeding between a miniature 'Zonal' and an 'Ivy-leaved' pelargonium carried out by Canon Stringer in the 1970s. They are very popular, double-flowered and neatly shaped dwarf plants with a distinct zonal band on the leaves.

■ ABOVE
'DEACON FINALE'

A free-flowering, compact cultivar which is easy to grow, but less ready to branch if the growing tips are not pinched out. The flowers are an outstanding wine-crimson and a great reward for any effort. 'Finale' grows well and flowers most profusely when planted in a 13cm (5in) pot, which encourages the plants to grow to almost 20cm (8in) tall, slightly taller than most dwarf cultivars. An attractive plant for patios and terraces.

■ LEFT
'CORAL REEF'

All the 'Deacon' hybrids are compact, neat plants but this cultivar with its deep salmon-pink flowers is amongst the most popular. 'Coral Reef' was produced in 1970, and is taller than most 'Deacons', growing to almost 25cm (10in) tall. It is very versatile and can be grown in almost any well-lit situation.

■ LEFT
'DEACON MANDARIN'

Almost the last of the 'Deacon' cultivars, this variety was produced in 1978. The flowers are a vibrant, clear orange which lasts all summer long. Neat and compact, it will remain below 20cm (8in) tall, and makes an outstanding addition to any window box or windowsill collection.

Rosebud zonal pelargoniums

The flowers are double and are composed of a tight mass of petals so that they resemble a small rosebud. These plants were much more widely grown in the Victorian period, when they were known as 'noisette' pelargoniums. The flower heads, carried above the foliage on tall, wiry stems, are lovely for use in flower arrangements.

■ LEFT
'SCARLET RAMBLER'

A traditional cultivar which has stunning, tightly clustered blooms that are a vibrant scarlet. Growth is robust, erect and will attain 40cm (16in) in height. Planted into a flower border, a small group of plants will provide cut flowers and colour throughout the summer.

■ BELOW
'PLUM RAMBLER'

Similar to 'Scarlet Rambler', the flowers of this variety are a most unusual plum colour. Plants tend to be rather leggy and require careful pinching out. An unusual plant which merits cultivation in a decorative patio pot or tub.

■ LEFT
'APPLE BLOSSOM ROSEBUD'

A popular cultivar which arose in the 1870s. The flowers are double, pale pink, flushed deeper pink, and are tightly clustered into dense heads. Plants require early pinching out to develop a bushy shape, then growth is robust and erect and will attain 35cm (14in) in height. This is a lovely flower for a border plant in dry climates, or a conservatory plant where the weather is moist.

Coloured leaf zonal pelargoniums

Plants with coloured leaves provide interest throughout the year. Several cultivars of pelargonium are grown almost exclusively for their beautiful leaves which can be green, golden, or silvery cream with red or dark zonal bands. Most of these plants are slow growing and some are very difficult to maintain. The colour of the leaves is usually improved by good natural light conditions, but most of these plants do not thrive in direct sunlight.

■ LEFT
'MR HENRY COX'

An old variety from 1879, which is still amongst the best and most popular of those grown today. The foliage is strongly tri-coloured, with a brilliant golden margin surrounding a green centre, overlaid by a deep red-black zone. The flowers are single, salmon-pink coloured. Plants are slow growing and require pinching out when young; they will reach 30cm (12in) in height. An exciting plant to grow as a standard or a specimen in a conservatory pot. It is not easy to propagate – take care when watering at the cutting stage.

■ LEFT
'ASHFIELD JUBILEE'

A glowing, golden-leaved variety which is naturally self-branching but slow growing. Plants will eventually attain 30cm (12in) in height and will flourish in a location which receives light during the early morning and late afternoon rather than the bright light of midday. The golden colour of the leaves will enliven any slightly shaded spot in a flower border, conservatory or patio.

■ BELOW
'MRS PARKER'

Known as a stellar-leaf zonal, the colouration of this cultivar will bring a lift to any planting scheme. The leaves have a grey-green centre surrounded by a white or pale cream border above which are held the double, rose-pink flowers. The plants are easy to propagate and are vigorous growers. They attain 45–55cm (18–22in) in height and are valuable for bedding schemes.

■ OPPOSITE BOTTOM LEFT
'HAPPY THOUGHT'

A highly unusual, variegated cultivar which arose in 1877. The leaves are rounded with reversed colouration, so that the centre is pale cream or yellow-green, edged with an irregular and often pale brown zone, all surrounded by a broad, bright green margin. Plants are erect, growing to 40–45cm (16–18in) tall, with thin, medium- to long-jointed stems. The flowers are small, single and crimson and are borne in small heads on long stems. This is a popular bedding variety which is easy to propagate.

■ OPPOSITE BOTTOM RIGHT
'LASS O'GOWRIE'

One of the older cultivars, it has been popular and widely grown since 1860. The leaves are tri-coloured, with a silver-cream margin surrounding a green centre, overlaid with a dark, reddish band; the flowers are single, scarlet and very striking above the foliage. Pinching out the growing point will encourage branching. The growth is naturally short at around 25–30cm (10–12in). The plants are easy to propagate and make an impressive display in a tub.

Regal pelargoniums

'Regals' have been popular as house and conservatory plants since the Victorian period; they can tolerate fairly shaded conditions, and are able to maintain growth even during the winter months. Except in the warmer states of America and in Australia, their flower and foliage characteristics make them generally unsuitable for use as bedding or border plants, although they will make good container plants outside.

■ LEFT
'BLACK MAGIC'
In the summer flush this cultivar is completely covered with rich, almost black, velvety flowers. The compact form and bushy growth to 35cm (14in) tall make this a winning plant for use in a window box or in a pot on a windowsill.

■ ABOVE
'RIMFIRE'

A popular modern cultivar, its almost black flowers have a deep red fire-like rim around the margin of each petal. The compact habit and bushy growth to 35cm (14in) in height make this an ideal plant for growing on a windowsill.

■ LEFT
'ASHLEY STEPHENSON'

A modern cultivar which has a lovely compact habit and few cultural problems. The flowers are creamy pink with a white throat, the upper petals have a mahogany blotch and the lower petals a larger, mahogany blaze. Masses of flowers are produced early in the summer, and fewer in a repeat flush later. A lovely plant for use as a single specimen in a decorative pot.

■ RIGHT

'FLEUR D'AMOUR'

A lovely plant, with leaves which are slightly paler than those of other 'Regals', and act as a good foil to the large, soft pink-and-white, frilly flowers. Growing to 35cm (14in) tall, this is a rewarding plant for almost any situation.

■ ABOVE

'MARGARET WAITE'

A compact, bushy variety which presents few problems and grows readily into a stunning display plant. The flowers are variable in shades of red, orange and salmon; the upper petals have a mahogany blotch and the lower petals a larger, mahogany blaze. A good repeat bloomer which enlivens any location either in a conservatory or garden pot.

■ RIGHT

'SUNRISE'

This cultivar was raised by William Schmidt in the USA. The flowers are very large, salmon-orange with a white throat, the upper petal blazed with magenta. Growth is normally up to 40cm (16in) in height, but plants can be grown to a standard over two years and are then very striking.

Angel pelargoniums

'Angel' pelargoniums became popular during the 1930s, in response to the exciting cultivars produced by the English hybridist, Langley Smith. Most 'Angels' grow as small, shrubby plants, with slender stems which can be encouraged into dense growth by frequent pinching out. The flowers are small, open, pansy-like in appearance and are usually produced in great numbers; removal of spent flowers will extend the flowering season.

■ ABOVE LEFT
'CATFORD BELLE'

Amongst the earliest of the 'Angels', this is a good example of a Langley Smith cultivar. Plants grow as compact shrubs, producing many small, mauve-purple flowers. The petals are slightly frilled and marked with purple. This is a wonderful cultivar for growing as a specimen plant in a decorative conservatory pot or urn.

■ RIGHT
'MOON MAIDEN'

Produced in 1984, 'Moon Maiden' reflects the work that has gone into extending the flowering season of the 'Angel' cultivars. The flowers are almost circular, light rose-coloured, marked with deeper pink, held above the neat, dark green leaves. Plants will grow to approximately 45–50cm (18–20in) tall. This is a wonderfully reliable plant, suitable for those starting a collection, or for any grower wanting a reliable, long-lasting display.

■ ABOVE RIGHT
'JER'REY'

This cultivar was raised in the late nineteenth century in Britain. It was recently rediscovered in the USA. It will undoubtedly become very popular due to the arresting flowers and full, bushy habit of the plant. Plants will grow to 35cm (14in) tall, and carry masses of deep red-purple flowers which have a picotee, crimson edge to the petals. The plant has an extended flowering period.

Decorative pelargoniums

Popular in the Victorian period, these are now something of an unrecognized group, and plants are often listed in directories and manuals under the 'Regal' or 'Angel' sections. They are certainly not 'Angels', as they have arisen from different parents, and in fact most of them are indeed old-fashioned 'Regals', differing from the modern varieties in the small size of their leaves and flowers.

'SANCHO PANZA'

This is an old cultivar, reintroduced in 1954 by Anthony Ayton and still popular. Plants form a compact, neat shrub with dark leaves. The flowers are deep purple, with a paler, lavender border. Plants will flower well in semi-shade, and are attractive to bees and other insects. They bring a sumptuous wealth to any garden when planted in a mass as bedding or in window boxes or tubs.

■ ABOVE
'MADAME LAYAL'

A highly attractive cultivar first grown in France, during the 1870s. This old favourite produces a wonderful show of bi-coloured flowers which have deep plum-purple upper petals, edged with white and white lower petals marked with dark purple. The plant can grow to 45cm (18in) tall, and will flourish under most conservatory conditions. Several pots plunged together into a large basket will create a wonderful Victorian atmosphere on a balcony or terrace.

■ LEFT
'BLACK KNIGHT'

A pretty cultivar which carries masses of small flowers. The flowers are dark purple-black, each petal edged with lavender. Shorter than most others in this group, plants will reach 40cm (16in) tall. It is ideal as a centrepiece for a mixed planting in a patio container or decorative pot.

Scented leaf pelargoniums

Scented pelargoniums are mainly grown for the wonderful, rich fragrances released from the leaves when they are touched, warmed by the sun, or bruised as you brush past them. Few of these varieties have large or brightly coloured flowers; they are often closely allied to basic species plants and carry simple, species-like, primitive flowers.

■ LEFT
'LADY SCARBOROUGH'

A variety of *P. crispum*, this is often known as the 'Curled-leaved Cranesbill' and was identified in the 1800s. The leaves are small, undulating and slightly crispy. They release a sweet rose-lemon scent when warm or bruised. Growth is spreading, rather than upright, and plants will eventually form a loose mound of scented leaves almost 50cm (20in) across. The flowers are small and pale pink, with darker purple veins. This is a great plant to grow in a traditional clay pot, placed in a dry, sunny position on a doorstep.

■ ABOVE
'LITTLE GEM'

A variety of the horticultural cultivar *P.* 'graveolens', which was first catalogued in 1910. The leaves are soft-textured, deeply lobed, toothed and release a warm, rose-lemon scent, above which the small mauve flowers are freely produced. Plants form a compact, bushy mound, spreading to 45cm (18in) and are very popular for cultivation in conservatories and on small balconies. Plants can also be used in a hanging basket, from which they will release their lovely scent.

■ ABOVE
'FRAGRANS'

A delightful plant both for its habit and for its scent. The leaves are grey-green and have a clean, refreshing pine scent. The flowers are small, white, borne on long, trailing, willowy stems but are themselves small and almost inconspicuous. Plants form a lax, open shrub, with semi-erect stems which grow to 20–25cm (8–10in) tall. This plant is ideal for growing as a pot plant indoors where the light is bright, as the scented leaves will clear the air better than any air-freshener.

Uniques

'Uniques' are usually large, shrubby
plants which have aromatic leaves
and bright, small flowers. They were
very popular in Victorian times, and
the cultivars available today are only
a handful of the range that were
then available.

'Uniques' make excellent pot and
patio plants, producing masses of
flowers in an early season flush. They
are generally easy plants to grow,
although sometimes prone to whitefly
infestations. Use a large container or
pot to ensure a good root-run and to
balance the shrubby top growth.

The plants are much improved
when grown outdoors and the whitefly problems are minimized too. Feed
outdoor plants regularly with high
potash liquid tomato food.

■ ABOVE
'PINK AURORE'S UNIQUE'

A pretty cultivar which has a robust, upright habit and grows to almost 50cm (20in) tall.
The flowers are camellia-rose pink, the upper petals have a burgundy blaze. A splendid
plant for use in the flower border or in a patio planter.

■ RIGHT
'ROLLISSON'S UNIQUE'

A delightful, compact plant, introduced
before 1880. The leaves release a pleasant
rose scent when bruised or warmed by
the sun. The flowers are magenta-purple,
which have broad, deeper purple markings
on the upper petals. Plants are tall
growing, and will attain 40–45cm
(16–18in) or more with a lax habit. This
cultivar is often considered to be a difficult
one to grow, although when you find the
right position, well grown specimen plants
make a very attractive display.

Stellar pelargoniums

This is an interesting group of 'Zonal' pelargoniums of which the early varieties were bred in Australia by Ted Both from *Pelargonium staphysagroides* and *P. × hortorum*. They have maple-shaped leaves marked with a dark zonal band. The flowers can be either single or double, with broad, serrated lower petals and narrow, forked upper petals. 'Stellars' are usually slow growing. They need to be kept drier than usual and positioned in a well-lit location.

■ LEFT
'FANDANGO'

Sometimes listed as 'Stellar Fandango', this is a striking cultivar from Australia. It has almost unzoned green leaves which act as a foil to the salmon-pink flowers. Growth is short-jointed and compact, to 18cm (7in) tall, and the flower heads are full and lifted above the leaves. Superb when grown in a garden tub either as a single plant or in a mixed planting.

■ ABOVE
'SUNRAYSIA'

A pretty cultivar which has only lightly zoned leaves and scarlet, single flowers. Plants will grow to 20cm (8in) tall, and are very versatile. They can be grown in containers for indoors or outside or used in bedding schemes in a flower border or on a rockery.

■ LEFT
'STRAWBERRY FAYRE'

Among the larger cultivars of the group, 'Strawberry Fayre' is popular for its almost constant flowering throughout the summer months. The flowers are single/double, coral-scarlet with a white eye. Plants will grow to almost 25cm (10in) in height.

■ ABOVE
'BIRD DANCER'

Introduced from Australia, this is a neat, miniature
'Stellar', which has attractively zoned leaves each
marked with a strong, dark band following the margin.
The flowers are single, pale pink, spidery with
narrow petals. A really delightful plant, growing to
20cm (8in) tall, which is very popular for cultivation
in pots on windowsills and in conservatories.

■ ABOVE
'RADS STAR'

A delightful cultivar which has almost uniformly green leaves on
which the zonal band is scarcely visible. They act as a good base
for the clear, rose-pink single flowers which have a white eye.
Plants will grow to almost 20cm (8in) tall and look gorgeous
grown *en masse* in a window box or patio tub.

■ RIGHT
'MEADOWSIDE MIDNIGHT'

A very unusual cultivar which has highly attractive dark brown,
almost black, leaves with only a very narrow green margin. The
flowers are orange, single, with slightly rounded petals. Plants are
slow growing and will attain 18cm (7in) in height. Requiring a
well-lit location in dry conditions, plants are best grown in pots
or urns where the soil moisture can be controlled.

Ivy-leaved pelargoniums

'Ivy-leaved' pelargoniums – often known as 'basket' or 'trailing' pelargoniums – were developed almost 300 years ago. They are probably the most easily grown of all pelargoniums, able to resist fairly low winter temperatures, and to enjoy the summer heat. Their versatile and robust habit makes them almost the most popular group of pelargoniums grown today.

■ LEFT
'RIO GRANDE'

A modern cultivar, introduced in 1982, which has made a strong impact due to the unusual flower colour. The flowers are double, deep maroon, almost black, with a white underside to each petal. The stems are short-jointed and carry small, shiny, bright green leaves. This cultivar mixes well with other plants or is interesting enough to grow on its own in a pot or urn.

■ LEFT
'ECLIPSE'

A popular cultivar which can be relied upon for masses of colour. The flowers are single, salmon-pink and produced in large open heads. Widely grown for use in hanging baskets.

■ OPPOSITE BOTTOM LEFT
'RIGI'

A wonderful, strong-growing plant which was introduced in 1932. The leaves are waxy, slightly undulating, with pointed lobes; the flowers are semi-double, cerise-pink with burgundy feathering on the upper petals. Plants benefit from cultivation over several years, and when established present a colourful display throughout the warm months. The robust nature of this variety makes it suitable for use as ground cover in a garden bed or on dry, stony ground.

■ OPPOSITE BOTTOM RIGHT
'GOLDEN LILAC GEM'

An ornamental cultivar which has golden leaves. The flowers are double, lilac, and are freely produced throughout the summer months. Plants have an almost dwarf habit, with short-jointed trailing stems, and are suitable for growing outside in all types of containers.

■ ABOVE
'HARVARD'

An American cultivar which has been grown since the 1970s. The flowers are semi-double, deep wine-red, and the leaves are remarkably rounded. The stems are long-jointed and can be used to festoon an archway or other framework.

■ ABOVE
'GIROFLEE'

A surprising cultivar, which brings together the leaves and trailing habit of the group, with almost rosebud-like flowers, which are double, bright purple, and crowded together in large, ball heads. A lovely plant to grow trailing over the wall of a raised bed, or large tub, where the flowers are easily visible.

Starting a collection

Take care when starting a
pelargonium collection; fascination
with the group will soon develop
and before long you will aspire to
growing every lovely pelargonium
which comes your way. Try to limit
yourself to growing only a few plants
at first, so that you can be sure
to handle and observe each one
regularly and so spot any signs of
stress or infection at an early stage.
Unattended, many cultivars will
grow into rather disappointing
plants, which can be easily avoided
by a little regular maintenance.

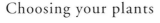

Choosing your plants

The different groups of pelargoniums
require different cultural care, so
restrict your collection to one group
until you are happily growing strong
and healthy plants, before branching
out into a wider range.

A visit to a specialist nursery or
pelargonium show will give you a
good idea of what to expect when
purchasing pelargoniums. Examine
the plant before purchase to check
that it is healthy, and that the young
stems have been pinched-out to
encourage a good form. Lift the
plant gently from the pot to look at
the root system, without disturbing

■ LEFT AND
BELOW
Choose healthy
plants which
show good, even
growth. Look
carefully at the
stems, leaves and,
if possible, the
roots, to make
sure the plants
are not infected
with any rot or
insect pests.

■ RIGHT
Planted in tubs and pots, pelargoniums thrive in open, sunny conditions.

the compost (potting soil); pale, young roots should be visible on the surface of the compost.

Pots and compost

When choosing pots in which to grow plants, it is important to think about cleanliness, about drainage and watering and to consider the ease with which the full pot can be moved. Both clay and plastic pots have recommendations. Plastic pots are easy to clean, light to handle and

■ ABOVE
A poorly growing plant, developing uneven growth and with yellow leaves and spent flowers left unremoved.

durable; clay pots, on the other hand, are porous, which reduces the risk of the compost becoming waterlogged. They have a natural quality which complements many plants, but full pots are heavy to move. Finally, any pot or container should be durable, and should have plenty of holes in the base to ensure good drainage through the compost.

Most pelargoniums grow well in the commercially available composts which are prepared for use in pots and containers, and which tend to be slightly acid. Take care to avoid composts prepared specially for cacti or other lime-loving plants. The final choice concerning the compost should be made only after the

container or pot has been decided upon. Soil or loam-based composts are heavy to handle, but tend to have a good reserve of plant nutrients and seem to encourage a slow rate of growth which supports flower production; soilless composts (growing mediums) based on coconut coir or other fibrous material are light to handle, but more care is required over watering and feeding plants.

Stand the plants out, so that each has enough space, and avoid crowding the plants so they touch each other. Encourage young plants to grow into good, bushy specimens by allowing each enough room to grow outwards, not just upwards.

Routine maintenance and cultivation

Before you start to grow any plant, it is always helpful to understand how and where the plants grow in their wild form. Most species of *Pelargonium* originate from arid, warm-temperate or subtropical regions, which are not usually exposed to frosts. They grow in full sun or part shade, in gravel-rich or well drained soils which are not constantly wet.

In cultivation, where winter temperatures drop below freezing and where the rainfall is plentiful, pelargoniums are best grown in pots or containers so that the compost (potting soil) moisture can be controlled, and so they may be moved under cover for frost protection. In some regions, such as in parts of California and Australia, which are climatically similar to their native conditions, many pelargoniums thrive as permanent herbaceous plants, in garden beds.

Light

All pelargoniums require bright light for strong growth and flowering. In greenhouses or conservatories, plants flourish in the light, but may need some shade protection from the high sun of summer. On windowsills and

REMOVING BROWN LEAVES

Using your thumb and index finger, carefully remove the yellow or brown leaves at the base of the petiole.

PINCHING OUT

Using the tips of your thumb and index finger, carefully remove the growing tip of each shoot.

indoors, pelargoniums need to be close to south-facing windows, east- or west-facing positions are less satisfactory. Plants receiving light from one direction only should be turned regularly to encourage even growth.

Hygiene

Careful cultivation and good hygiene are most important during the winter months, when low light levels and cooler temperatures reduce the rate of growth. High atmospheric humidity at this time encourages fungal infections and plants are prone to rot. The removal of dead leaves and spent flowers throughout the year is important, especially for 'Angel' and 'Regal' cultivars where the growth is compact. Dead leaves and flowers left on a plant are prime sites for the start of fungal rots and insect pest infestations.

Pinching out

Pinching out involves removing the growing tip from the stem. This is of particular importance for young plants to encourage a good shape from the start.

Watering

Most *Pelargonium* species naturally have long, searching roots as an adaptation to their dry environment. When grown in pots, the roots are restricted and the plants need frequent watering. Similarly, pelargonium cultivars are thirsty plants, but like the species, they prefer to be grown drier rather than wet. Plants will recover well from a period when they have been too dry, but overwatering will kill them. When a large number of plants are

To re-wet completely dry potting compost (potting soil), plunge the whole pot into a bucket of water, so that only the leafy top remains out of the water. Leave the plant until the pot stops releasing air bubbles, then lift it and stand it to drain.

grown, an automatic watering system should be considered, such as individual drip units for each pot, or standing the pots on capillary matting which is regularly flooded.

Feeding

Fresh potting compost (potting soil), especially loam or soil-based ones, contain some nutrients which will maintain healthy, active growth for approximately three months after potting. This time is greatly reduced for soilless composts (growing mediums). After this initial period, plants should be fed regularly throughout the growing period – a little and often is the best maxim. During dry months, when you may need to water containers almost every day, use a liquid feed at half-strength on every other (alternate) watering; if the weather has been very wet and you are hardly watering at all, apply a granular feed around the base of the plants, following the manufacturer's recommendations. This way, fertilizer will be released slowly into the soil or compost with the rain water.

Granular or fertilizer pellets can be useful for feeding 'Ivy-leaved' cultivars, especially if they are growing in situations difficult to

A tomato fertilizer diluted as recommended can be used to feed your 'Regal' pelargonium cultivars. Water the solution on to the compost (potting soil) on every fifth watering.

water. Position the pellet just below the surface of the potting compost.

Different pelargonium groups require different nutrient levels, so take care to give the correct fertilizer to each of your plants. All the 'Regal' pelargoniums, 'Unique' and ornamental-leaved 'Zonal' cultivars, need fertilizers high in potassium to develop healthy flowers. A special tomato fertilizer is ideal for these plants, so check that the fertilizer nutrient ratio you use is shown as 1:1:2 N:P:K (nitrogen:phosphate: potassium), or 1:0:2. Too high a level of potassium may cause the leaves to develop yellow patches between the veins, which is due to magnesium deficiency. This can be easily cured

RE-POTTING OLDER PLANTS

1 Make sure that the compost (potting soil) is dry, cradle the plant and the root-ball and carefully remove the pot from the plant.

2 Gently tease the rootball so that the compost crumbles and falls away from the roots. Remove two-thirds of the compost. Trim the roots with secateurs (pruners). Line the base of the pot with fresh compost.

3 Holding the plant with one hand, use the other to pour compost into the pot around the roots, as you gently lower the remaining rootball into the pot.

4 Firm any supporting canes into the fresh compost and water the pot well. Stand the pot in a lightly shaded, sheltered position until new roots have developed.

by watering the plants with a solution of Epsom salts at the rate of 1g per litre (1oz per 5 gals). The other groups will flourish on fertilizers high in nitrogen, so use a general fertilizer which has the ratio 1:1:1. Lush pelargoniums with soft leaves are particularly prone to rust disease.

Re-potting older plants

Re-potting is the term used for potting a mature plant into the same sized pot, or (rarely) in a slightly smaller pot. Prune away the top growth of the plant, to reduce the stress on the disturbed root system.

Preparing for winter

Pelargoniums need frost protection, so move them into well-lit conditions, under cover, in a greenhouse or on to south-facing windowsills. Prune the plants well to reduce their size and prevent cold damage.

Plants can also be stored, wrapped in newspaper, or buried in a dry insulating material. Prepare for this by removing the soft wood and leaves. Remove most of the potting compost (potting soil) from the roots. In the spring, trim the roots and re-pot the plants in small pots.

POTTING-ON

1 Potting-on is best carried out during the warm months. Lift the plant and rootball out of the pot; if the roots are clearly visible, potting-on is advised. Prepare the new pot. This should be slightly larger than the existing pot.

2 Line the base of the pot with fresh compost (potting soil).

3 Holding the plant between the fingers of your left hand and the pot in your right hand, turn the pot upside down, tapping the rim against the bench edge.

4 Turn the plant on to its side. Holding the top of the plant with the left hand, gently remove the pot from the rootball.

CUTTING BACK

5 Put the rootball into the prepared pot. Add more compost on top of the rootball, pressing it firmly down the sides with your forefingers.

6 Water the plant well. Getting the rootball thoroughly soaked at this stage will ensure that the plant takes up water properly in the future.

1 Use sharp secateurs (pruners) to cut back the stems by approximately two-thirds, working around the plant.

2 Make sure that you do not leave any torn or broken stems which will be an easy site for infection to enter.

Bedding

BEDDING PLANTS

'Beatrix'	'Irene'
'Bliss'	'Joan Fontaine'
'Bonanza'	'Mrs Parker'
'Coral Reef'	'Occold Shield'
'Freckles'	'Rose Irene'
'Happy Thought'	'Springtime'
PAC 'Ice Crystal'	

'Zonal' pelargoniums are often used for bedding and are sold as small plantlets in disposable pots or modules. To ensure a really good display, plan your scheme on paper, working out how many plants you need to develop a striking arrangement. The greatest impact will be achieved if you restrict yourself to using bold clumps of only one pelargonium variety in each location.

Different cultivars grow and flower at different rates and times, so mixed plantings appear patchy. Plant the bedding out as early as practicable so that the plants have as long a growing season as possible. If late frosts are frequent, either grow plantlets on, potted into individual pots and protected in a greenhouse or conservatory, or use some method to protect planted bedding from frost damage. Small cloches of glass or even cut plastic

bottles can be effective, as can sheets of special horticultural fleece or old net curtains draped over the plants at night.

Choose a site which has good light, with some full sunlight each day. Prepare the site in advance, but do not be tempted to incorporate too

much organic matter which will encourage leafy growth rather than flowers. As autumn approaches and frosts threaten, either lift and prune the plants or discard them (see Routine maintenance – preparing for winter). Alternatively, take cuttings to maintain your stock (see Propagation).

PELARGONIUMS FOR GROWING AS STANDARDS

'Apple Blossom Rosebud'
'Bliss'
'Deacon Finale'
'Lord Bute'
'Mrs Parker'

PLANTING BEDDING PLANTS

1 Prepare the planting site, removing any weeds; use a rake to remove any debris and stones and to level the surface.

2 Carefully water the plantlets, making sure that the compost (potting soil) is fully wet. Plants grown in soilless compost (growing medium) often become so dry that re-wetting is difficult.

GROWING A STANDARD PELARGONIUM

A standard plant is shaped rather like a small tree, with a straight stem and a bushy crown. Standard plants are a delightful and unusual way of growing pelargoniums, and will add immediate interest to any situation. The techniques involved are not difficult, and the result is well worth the effort. Almost all pelargonium cultivars can be trained as standards, but 'Zonal' or 'Regal' cultivars are the most suitable for beginners.

Ideally, the chosen cultivar should be one that will develop easily into an upright-growing plant and which has little tendency to branch. It is best to commence training from the earliest stage, choosing a tip cutting and growing this on without pinching out the growing point. Cuttings taken in early spring will have a long growing period during the warm months to develop a robust form.

Young plants should be grown against a stake right from the start. To keep the stem growing straight, tie it loosely to the stake at each leaf. All the side shoots which develop in the leaf angles must be pinched out as the stem grows upward; do not remove the leaves from the stem while they are green and healthy.

In the second season of growth, encourage the development of branches and a full, crowning head by regularly pinching out the growing tips.

3 Using a trowel, dig a hole for each plant. Pay attention to the spacing; plants should be approximately 20cm (8in) apart. Water each hole before you position the young plant.

4 Carefully remove the plants from the modules. Take care not to squash or compress the rootball.

5 Place the rootball into the hole, and gently push the soil around and over it. Firm the soil with your fingers. Water the freshly planted bedding to settle the soil around the roots.

Planting in a hanging basket

'Ivy-leaved' pelargoniums are ideal for a hanging basket or pot, either alone or as part of a mixed planting. The trailing stems of the pelargonium will cascade with lush greenery, mixing well with other plants and enlivening the whole arrangement with bright flowers. The stiff, shiny, almost waxy leaves of some of these pelargoniums resist the rigours of growing in a hanging container and present a fresh green appearance throughout the summer.

When designing a basket, remember to use multiples of the same variety to create a striking impact. Try to plant containers early in the year, during January–February in northern climates, if you can keep them frost-free.

In the basket we have used three different pelargoniums: *P.* 'Eclipse', an 'Ivy-leaved' cultivar which has single, pink flowers and good robust growth to get a strong, trailing effect; *P.* 'Happy Thought', which has

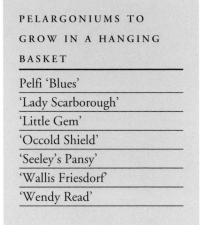

PELARGONIUMS TO GROW IN A HANGING BASKET

Pelfi 'Blues'
'Lady Scarborough'
'Little Gem'
'Occold Shield'
'Seeley's Pansy'
'Wallis Friesdorf'
'Wendy Read'

tri-coloured leaves and will provide interest before the flowers really get going; and the variegated, scented *P.* 'Lady Plymouth' as the centre plant, which will release a lovely aroma. We have also used a variegated ivy, trailing blue and white lobelias and the grey-leaved *Helichrysum petiolare* to get a full and generous effect. For a really impressive display, use as many plants as you can fit into the basket and feed and water it regularly.

To reduce the weight of a hanging container it is best to use a soilless compost (growing medium) which will be much lighter, especially when wet. Hanging containers always dry out rapidly, and can often be difficult to water, so add a water-retaining gel to the compost (potting soil).

1 Line the basket with an appropriate liner. We have used a water-permeable material which can be purchased by the metre.

2 Cut the liner to fit the basket.

3 Begin to fill the basket with compost (potting soil).

4 Add some perlite or vermiculite to the compost. This will both improve the drainage and reduce the weight of the basket.

5 Add water-retaining gel at the rate recommended by the manufacturer. Half fill the basket with this mixture.

6 When half full, make small holes in the sides, through the liner, to take the trailing plants around the base.

7 Push the trailing plants (*Lobelia* is being used here) through the holes.

8 Continue to fill the basket with the compost, perlite and water-retaining gel mix.

9 Position the remaining trailing plants around the edge of the basket, and in the centre, the coloured-leaved 'Happy Thought' with the scented-leaved 'Lady Plymouth'.

10 Gently take the plants out of their pots, and set them on to the bed of compost. Backfill around the plants with more compost.

11 Insert pellets of slow-release fertilizer at the rate recommended by the manufacturer.

12 Water the basket well and allow it to drain before hanging it in position.

Planting in a container

Pelargoniums are ideal plants for growing in pots and containers of all shapes and sizes. Free-standing pots will allow you to choose carefully the locations to suit the plants, and you can move smaller pots around the garden or patio to where you desire colour or as the weather dictates. Wall pots are an interesting way of adding colour at a high level in the garden.

One of the most important benefits of growing pelargoniums in a container is that you can control the soil or compost (potting soil) and its moisture content. Pelargoniums will thrive best in a well-drained, dry soil, and porous pots – clay, wood or

PELARGONIUMS TO GROW IN PATIO TUBS AND CONTAINERS	
'Ann Hoysted'	'Mrs Pollock'
'Bliss'	'Occold Shield'
'Coral Reef'	'Plum Rambler'
'Deacon Finale'	'Rose Irene'
'Freckles'	'Scarlet Unique'
PAC 'Ice Crystal'	'Wallis Friesdorf'

even woven baskets – will allow the soil mass to lose water easily through the sides of the container, which removes the danger of soggy compost and rotten roots (see Starting a collection – Pots and compost).

The restricted root-run of pots and containers influences the growth and flower production of the plant. Flowers are usually a precursor to seeds. Seeds are produced as a means of a plant spreading out into a new location. If there is no slight stress on your plant in its pot or container,

1 Broken pieces of polystyrene in the bottom of the container are an appropriate, light, drainage material for wall pots.

2 Put a layer of compost (soil mix) over the polystyrene, half filling the container. Use a light, soilless compost (growing medium) for wall pots.

3 Add water-retaining gel, following the manufacturer's recommendations. Mix this into the compost.

Grey *Helichrysum petiolare* is a wonderful foil to the pink blooms on this short-jointed 'ivy-leaved' pelargonium.

PELARGONIUMS FOR WINDOW BOXES
'Bliss'
Pelfi 'Blues'
'Coral Reef'
'Deacon Mandarin'
PAC 'Lovesong'
'Mr Everaarts'
'Occold Shield'
'Wallis Friesdorf'
'Wendy Read'

then there is little need for it to spread out in this way. If the container is much too large for a plant, and the roots have lots of space, it is likely that flowering will be reduced. The plant will be putting all its resources into root and stem production and little into flowering. As the roots become confined, causing some slight stress, flowering is encouraged, so choose the size of your container carefully, with consideration of growth and flowering.

4 Position the plants before removing their pots, so as not to damage the roots when handling. Put taller plants at the back, and trailing plants near the front.

5 Remove the pots; cover the rootballs with compost and push a fertilizer pellet into the top of the compost.

6 Water the container to settle the compost around the roots of the young plants.

Propagation

The propagation of most pelargoniums is not a difficult procedure. The majority of cultivars can be grown easily from cuttings, taken when the plants are in full and active growth.

It is vital to take great care when choosing plants from which to take cuttings. The young plants will most likely be a replicate of the parent plant, so only propagate your best and healthiest plants. Try to use non-flowering stems, because flowering weakens the plant. Always take a plentiful number of cuttings, so that you may choose and keep only the most vigorous and healthy.

Taking cuttings

Cuttings taken in late winter or in early spring will usually be sufficiently mature to flower during their first summer. Cuttings taken in late summer or early autumn will be well established before the cold winter months, and should pose no problems for over-wintering. Their small size will be beneficial when greenhouse space is restricted.

Cuttings should not be covered, but place the pots in a warm, humid situation such as in a greenhouse, making sure that they are not in

1 Before you make any cuts, prepare the rooting medium. Use individual pots or propagation cells and a special cuttings compost (potting soil) which is fertilizer-free and has good drainage. Drench the compost well, using a small mist sprayer.

2 Use a special propagation knife, which has a razor-sharp, flat blade, to make a clean, slanted cut, just above a node, so that the portion you remove is approximately 8cm (3in) long. Use the knife to neaten and trim any torn edges.

3 Carefully make a straight cut across the stem, just below the first node. The upper leaf (leaves) should be left in place.

4 The lower portions of the stem can then be cut into sections so that each cutting has a short length of stem just above and just below the node.

5 Roots will develop from the nodes at the base of the stems.

6 Fill a small pot with moist compost, make a hole in the centre, and insert so the node is in contact with the compost.

direct sunlight. Try to maintain
the soil temperature at about 23°C
(73°F). Spray the cuttings every day,
with plain water, or with a weak
fungicide solution if signs of
rot appear. The cuttings should
develop roots within three weeks,
although they will not all root at
the same rate, which is why
individual pots or propagation
cells are recommended.

When the cuttings are rooted, pot
them on into individual 8cm (3in)
pots, using a loam-based or soilless
compost (growing medium). Grow
these young plants on in the sheltered
conditions of the greenhouse or
propagating tray where they rooted
for approximately one week, as they
settle into the fresh compost.

Then harden the young plants off
by gradually, over a period of up to
three weeks or so, reducing the heat
and amount of shelter in stages.
For example, reduce the heat in the
propagator; then remove the cover;
then transfer the young plants to a
cool windowsill or greenhouse; then
move them into a coldframe which
can be left open for progressively
longer periods until it is left open all
day. Keep the plants covered at night
and don't plant them out until all
danger of frost is past.

Layering plants

Layering plants is easy and is
particularly suitable for plants
growing in garden beds and flower
borders or if propagation space is
restricted. No material is removed
from the parent plant until the roots
are formed and the young plant can
be self-supporting.

The simple method of layering
is most suitable for ivy-leaved
pelargoniums and for some of
the lax-growing species of scented
leaf pelargoniums.

Plants from seed

Pelargonium seed is available from
several seed companies. The seed is
usually F1 hybrid seed, the result of
a cross made between two inbred
cultivars. Seeds should be sown
during late July – early August for
flowering the following summer.

Seed produced on your own plants
can be collected for sowing; however,
only the seed produced on pure
species plants will result in true
replicate young plants. F1 hybrid
plants will not come true from seed,
and like all cultivars, these are best

LAYERING

1 Take one stem of the mature plant
and bend it downwards until it touches
the top of the compost (potting soil)
of the smaller pot (or the ground next to
the parent plant). At the point where the
stem meets the ground, scrape away a little
of the outer layer from the stem using a
blunt knife.

2 Use hair-pins or wire to pin the
stem firmly down, so that the scraped
parts of the stem are in close contact
with the compost. Water, and wait for
roots to grow.

■ LEFT
An attractive flower arrangement of pelargonium species which are best grown from seed.

propagated by cuttings. Seeds should be sown as soon as they are ripe, when the feathery appendage, or awn, curls and lifts the seed toward the top of the central column. Collect the seeds at this stage and dry them in a paper bag for 24 hours. To sow, press the seed, pointed end downward, into the compost, so that the awn is sticking up from the surface. This is important because the awn will swell with increasing humidity and push the small seed head down into the soil to the correct depth. Cover the seeds with cling film (plastic wrap).

Seedlings should appear within four or five days, although some seeds may be slower, so don't throw away the seed compost too quickly. Remove the cling film as soon as the seedlings appear, otherwise they will be encouraged to grow too softly and will be prone to rotting. Take care

not to keep the seedling compost too wet, and reduce the temperature to 18°C (65°F).

When the seedlings are 2.5cm (1in) tall, use a broad, flat instrument such as the rounded blade of a table knife to prick them out. Pricking out involves lifting each seedling, together with the soil around the young roots, from the seed tray compost and setting it carefully into fresh seedling compost, in an individual 6cm (2.5in) pot. Seedlings should be hardened off as for plants raised from cuttings (see Propagation).

PLANTING FROM SEED

1 Fill the seed tray with the prepared compost (potting soil) of equal parts seed compost and horticultural sand. Press the compost into the tray with a flat board, so that it is firm and the surface is flat. Stand the tray in a reservoir of water so that it is uniformly moist, without puddles on the surface. Drain it.

2 Carefully put the seeds from the packet individually on to the surface of the compost, spacing them approximately 2.5cm (1in) apart. Sieve (strain) a small quantity of compost and sand mixture over the seeds, so they are just covered.

3 Water the tray with a fungicide solution and then cover it with cling film (plastic wrap), to prevent it from drying out. The temperature should be controlled at 23°C (73°F).

Calendar

Spring

In warm climates, examine plants growing in garden beds for winter damage and for signs of pests or disease. Cut away any dead shoots, and treat any infections promptly. Plant new stock to replace old or lost plants. Fertilize and mulch all plants.

Examine pot plants for winter damage and for pests or diseases. Cut away dead shoots and infected ones. Increase watering to completely moisten each pot. Allow the compost (potting soil) to become almost dry before the next watering. Pot on all plants into clean pots using fresh compost. Start to shape plants by pinching out the tips.

Mature plants cut back in the autumn will have fresh growth, suitable for cuttings. Early spring cuttings grown with bottom heat of approximately 20°C (68°F) will grow into flowering plants for the summer. In early spring, take cuttings of 'Regals', 'Angels', 'Uniques' and 'Zonals', before they start to bud up, especially those intended for growing into standards next year.

Plant hanging baskets and decorative patio pots. Outdoors, prepare the ground for bedding and border plants.

■ ABOVE
Cuttings can be taken from the new growth of these mature zonal pelargoniums.

Late spring – early summer

Outdoors, plant out bedding after the last frost. Use small cloches to protect plants if frost threatens.

Develop a regular watering and feeding routine for pot plants. Check and examine each plant regularly.

Summer

Carefully watch conditions in greenhouses and conservatories. Create shade and ventilate to maintain air movement.

Monitor and treat pest or disease occurrence promptly. Treat infected plants before their flower buds open.

In late summer, sow seeds for next year's bedding, and take cuttings for use in next year's hanging baskets and pots. Dead-head all plants regularly.

Autumn

Remove any shade to expose pot plants to maximum levels of light. Check heating systems for frost protection.

Choose plants which will be discarded rather than maintained over winter. Take any cuttings you require to replace these. Reduce feeding and take care not to over-water. Move under cover all pots and containers, dig up bedding and pot up any plants which will be kept.

Take care with hygiene, remove all yellowing and dead leaves and flowers. Watch for fungal diseases. Decrease watering as growth slows; allowing the compost to become dry before re-wetting slightly. Prune any plants which will be kept over winter.

Winter

Monitor the maximum-minimum thermometer daily for temperature – watch overnight temperature levels.

Clean and ventilate greenhouses or conservatories.

Pests and diseases

Although pelargoniums are not prone to many troublesome pests or diseases, they do suffer from general fungal and insect attacks, as do other pot plants. The most important motto in pest and disease management is: 'Prevention is better than cure'. Healthy plants will resist any possible infections more easily, so attention to watering and feeding regimes will encourage strong and firm growth and reduce plant stress. Care taken over growing conditions – the creation of a clean and tidy environment through the removal of debris – will reduce the hiding and breeding places of pests. Finally, grow only a few plants, so that you can be sure to handle and observe each regularly and spot any signs of stress or infection at an early stage.

Aphids

How to identify: Greenfly are the most common and troublesome of the many aphids and are a particularly frequent pest of 'Ivy-leaved' cultivars. Greenfly usually cluster on the growing tips of the plant, causing them to become distorted. Most aphid infestations are usually accompanied by a black 'sooty mould' which grows on the

aphid's sugary excretion, known as honeydew, which falls on to the leaves of the infested plants. Root aphids may be a problem, usually on older pot plants, causing stunting and yellowing of the growth. They are apparent as small, pale insects clustered on the roots of the plant.
Cause: Plants grown under stress.
Control: Physical removal of infested plant parts will give some control. In greenhouses or conservatories use predator insects, such as ladybirds, which can be purchased in bulk and will help to prevent major pest outbreaks. When infestation becomes a problem, use an insecticidal 'soft soap' which is effective and benign to other insects. Sooty moulds can be easily washed off the leaves. Treat root aphids by drenching the compost (potting soil) with aphid insecticide.

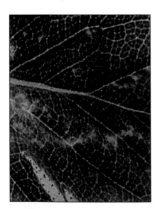

Aphid

Blackleg

How to identify: Damage appears firstly at soil level, as a collar around the base of the plant. Young cuttings and soft young plants are prone to this fungal disease, particularly amongst the 'Zonal' cultivars.
Cause: Infection is through soil-borne spores and damage appears firstly at soil level.
Control: Infected cuttings should be discarded, together with the compost (potting soil). There is no highly successful treatment against this disease, so preventive action such as a general fungicidal drench for cuttings and young plants is recommended.

Botrytis

How to identify: Infection is easily recognized as a grey, hair-like mould on soft green stems or on flowers and leaves.

Botrytis

Cause: Infection by *Botrytis* fungi is the result of overcrowding and overly wet compost (potting soil), and most often occurs in late winter or early spring when growth is slow and air circulation is reduced.
Control: Care over cultural hygiene and attention to ventilation can be effective in the prevention of this disease. Spray or powder applications of systemic chemical fungicides can also be helpful, but remember to alternate any chemical treatment to avoid development of resistance.

Pelargonium rust

How to identify: Infection occurs first on the undersides of the leaves, appearing as small, circular yellow spots which then become larger and darker with the

Pelargonium rust

production of spores. The spores spread on air currents, through contact and water splash. This is a serious disease, particularly affecting 'Zonal' cultivars.
Cause: Rust is rife in damp, still conditions, both in greenhouses and outside, particularly on plants with soft leaves.
Control: Rapid removal and destruction of all infected parts can be partially effective, accompanied by improved ventilation and reduced watering. Fungicidal spray can be effective, but treatments should be alternated.

Red spider mites

How to identify: The leaves become dull looking and silvery bronze on the underside, and they soon wither and fall. Severe infestations are obvious due to the fine webs which develop between the remaining shoots.
Cause: The mites thrive in the hot, dry atmosphere most beneficial to pelargoniums.
Control: Deter by spraying the plants, especially the undersides of the leaves, regularly with water. Any infected plant should be rapidly isolated, either destroyed or treated with a systemic miticide. In greenhouses, the biological predator *Phytoseiulus persimimilis* is a successful means of control.

Vine weevils

How to identify: Sudden wilting and death of the plants which, when examined, show that the roots have been cut and destroyed. Damage is caused by the vine weevil larvae which feed on roots from late summer onwards.

The larvae are visible in the compost (potting soil), and all new plants should be checked before introduction to a collection. The adult weevils are only damaging because of the vast number of the eggs that they lay in the soil of garden beds or pots.
Control: Always check the compost (potting soil) of new pot plants before you introduce them into a collection. Once infestation has been identified, then biological control is the best solution – a minute worm or nematode can be watered into the soil and will search out the larvae, and effectively feed on them. Marketed as Nemyss or Nemyss H, treatment can be carried out when soil temperatures are at least 10°C (50°F).

Whitefly

How to identify: Most obvious in the adult phase as small, white moth-like insects, which fly briefly when disturbed. Found most frequently on the undersides of the leaves, both adults and immature stages feed on the sap of the leaf cells. Like other aphids, they excrete a sugar-rich honeydew which soon becomes mould-infected and turns black, soiling the leaves. They are the most problematic

pelargonium pest, and are particularly common on 'Unique' and 'Regal' cultivars. Whiteflies breed rapidly and infestations develop very quickly.
Control: Whitefly are difficult to eradicate and have developed immunity to many insecticides. Sticky, yellow insect sheets can be hung between the plants to trap whitefly, and these should be examined frequently. In greenhouses, whitefly can be treated by biological control using a small wasp – *Encarsia formosa* – as a predator, or by MYCOTAL, an infective fungus. It is not possible to mix biological and chemical treatments. If insecticidal sprays are used, applications should be alternated, using at least two different sprays, and care must be taken not to spray in bright weather which will cause the leaves to scorch.

Red spider mite

Vine weevil and its larvae

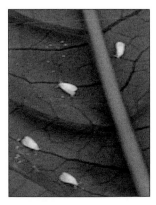

Whitefly

Other recommended pelargoniums

'**Ann Hoysted**' A striking 'Regal' due to the particularly large blooms it carries throughout the early summer. The flowers are dark red, the upper petals almost black. Compact and neat, plants will grow up to 45cm (18in) tall, and like others in this group will do best in a 15cm (6in) pot. Splendid as a central plant in a mixed patio urn.

'**Aztec**' Introduced from the USA in 1962, this was once a favourite 'Regal' variety for exhibition growing. Plants are naturally self branching, with a sturdy habit, growing to 40cm (16in) tall, with attractively shaped leaves which are slightly paler green than most pelargoniums in this group. The flowers are white with strawberry and bronze markings on each petal. Plants are compact and bushy and exceptionally free flowering.

'**Fringed Aztec**', developed in 1977, is a unique sport from 'Aztec', and carries flowers of a similar colour to the parent, but each petal is fringed.

'**Beatrix**' A marvellous double-flowered plant which forms a compact bush, up to 30cm (12in) tall, and holds its fuchsia-purple heads of flowers well above the leaves. The flower tone makes this a suitable cultivar wherever strong colour is required.

'**Bonanza**' A vivid double-flowered cultivar which was released in 1970. The plants are bushy and compact, carrying neon-rose pink

'Ann Hoysted'

flowers in full, open heads. Ideal for use as bedding plants, individuals will grow to 15–20cm (6–8in) tall with a broader, leafy spread.

'**Carisbrook**' Amongst the earliest 'Regal' cultivars grown, this plant has been popular since the mid-nineteenth century. The flowers are large, pink with maroon markings. Plants are leggy, attaining 45cm (18in) in height, but are easily grown and suitable for beginners.

'**Chelsea Gem**' An old variety, developed in 1880, which has proved itself as a useful bedding plant and a striking pot plant. Growing as a robust bush, up to 40cm (16in) tall, this cultivar branches well and carries attractive silvery green

leaves which have a cream margin. The pale pink, double flowers are freely produced. Plants have a tendency to become leggy once flowering has commenced, but can be pinched-out to encourage branching.

'**Crimson Unique**' An old variety which was raised around the mid-nineteenth century. Plants will attain a mature height and spread of 45–50cm (18–20in). The leaves are pungent, below bright, crimson flowers which are each marked with deep, almost black feathering. 'Crimson Unique' is suitable for partially shaded locations, and it will even make an impact positioned at the back of a flower border.

'Beatrix'

'**Crowfield**' A super miniature cultivar, which appears to be almost swamped by its blooms. The flowers are single/double, carmine pink,

and produced in profusion. A lovely plant for use in window boxes or on windowsills.

'**Freak of Nature**' This ornamental-leaved cultivar was introduced in 1880. It is very striking because it has reversed colouration: the stems, leaf petioles and flower stalks are white, and the leaves each have an irregular green margin. Growth is compact, bushy, up to 25cm (10in) tall, and the flowers are single, red, and striking against the foliage.

'**Freckles**' A seed-raised, really striking single-flowered variety from the sub-section known as 'Speckled Geraniums'. The flowers, pink, speckled with dark red splashes and dots, are arranged in large clusters almost 12cm (5in) across and presented above green leaves which carry a strongly marked dark zonal band. Plants need pinching-out to become really bushy, but the impact of the flowers will reward all efforts. Growth is up to 30cm (12in) in height, and this variety is most suited to growing in pots, tubs and containers where the flowers are easily admired.

PAC '**Ice Crystal**' Also controlled under Plant Breeders' Rights, this is an eye-catching cultivar which carries semi-double mauve flowers, feathered with lavender, with a more solid, lavender blotch on the lower petals. Splendid plants for use as a centre-piece for hanging baskets or in a mixed, high impact patio planter.

'Imperial Butterfly' Introduced in 1989, this 'Angel' cultivar has delightful, lemon-scented leaves and carries masses of white flowers, each feathered with purple. Plants will grow to 45cm (18in) tall and are suitable for patio or conservatory planters.

'Kleine Liebling' Often listed as 'Petit Pierre', this lovely, miniature plant is enhanced by its bushy habit and pale green leaves. The flowers are single, small and pink. Several plants will grow well together in a pretty basket or windowsill pot.

'Bonanza'

'Lady Plymouth' Amongst the earliest varieties arising from the horticultural cultivar *P.* 'graveolens', 'Lady Plymouth' was first described

in 1800. This is one of the most popular scented leaf pelargoniums, which has very pretty, silver leaves that release a strongly medicinal, pungent

'Crimson Unique'

aroma. The lilac-mauve flowers are small but in many-flowered clusters. Use for bedding, conservatory or greenhouse cultivation.

'Lord Bute' An older, very popular 'Regal' cultivar, which was produced towards the end of the nineteenth century. The flowers are small but stunning, produced in large clusters, the petals almost black, velvety, with a picotee pink edge to each. Being an older cultivar, plants grow tall, to almost 45cm (18in). This is an ideal feature plant for a flower border.

'Madame Layal' A highly attractive 'Decorative' cultivar first grown in France during the 1870s. This old favourite produces a wonderful show of

bi-coloured flowers which have deep plum-purple upper petals, edged with white and white lower petals marked with dark purple. The entire plant can grow to 45cm (18in) tall, and will flourish under most conservatory conditions. Several pots plunged together into a large basket will create a wonderful Victorian atmosphere on a balcony or terrace patio.

'Mrs Pollock' The 'Zonal' pelargonium , 'Mrs Pollock' has been a favourite since 1858. The tri-coloured leaves have a rich cream margin surrounding the green centre and dark red zonal band. The single flowers are orange-red with a small white eye. A strong-growing cultivar, plants will attain 35cm (14in) in height, and are a reliable addition to a flower border or container.

'Old Spice' Scented leaf pelargonium 'Old Spice' is a hybrid between *P. odoratissimum* and *P.* × *fragrans*, which was raised in the 1960s. The leaves are small and rounded and release a spicy aroma. Plants form a compact, neat mound only 25cm (10in) high. A versatile plant suitable for growing in a window box, or a herb garden, or as a corner plant in a bedding scheme in a good, sunny position.

'Patricia Andrea' A strong-growing 'Zonal' pelargonium introduced in 1967, which is often listed under the sub-section 'Tulip Flowered Zonals'. The flowers are deep carmine pink, and never open fully, so resembling small tulip flowers. The flower texture is firm, almost waxy, and they are long-lasting, which makes them popular for use in flower arrangements. Plants will grow to almost 40cm (16in) tall and are striking when grown in tubs, urns or as specimens in decorative pots.

Pelargonium peltatum A variable plant which grows wild in the Cape Province and the Natal region of South Africa. The stems are often slightly angular, almost succulent,

'Crowfield'

climbing or trailing through vegetation and bearing round, waxy, somewhat aromatic leaves. Stems can grow to 2m (7ft) or more in length.

The flowers are white, pink or pale purple and when crushed yield a deep blue dye, which has been used as a natural colourant in painting.

'Diane Palmer'

'Plenty' Known as a 'bird's egg' variety, this 'Zonal' cultivar is one of a group which originated in the late nineteenth century in France. 'Plenty' carries semi-double, white flowers with a scattering of fine pink spots. Plants tend to be a bit leggy, growing to about 25cm (10in) tall, with medium-small leaves which are not strongly marked. Cultivars in this group can be found in specialist nurseries and collections, and are best grown as conservatory plants.
'Regina' A superb, double-flowered cultivar developed in 1964, which is famous throughout the pelargonium world as a show winner. It is the parent of many modern

cultivars, passing on its compact, short-jointed and bushy habit. Plants will grow to 35cm (14in) tall. The flowers are a wonderful pale pink, deepening to coral in the centre. They are borne in large, dense heads which make a striking impact when the plant is used for summer bedding. Excellent for cut flowers.
'Royal Ascot' A delightful, established 'Decorative' cultivar which forms a good-looking plant. The flowers are large, crimson, the upper petals overlaid with wine feathering and the whole lit by a white throat. Growing to 50cm (20in) tall, this cultivar is suitable for planting as a group in a flower border.

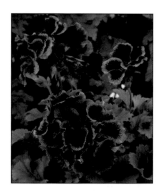

'Fareham'

'Rita Scheen' A silver leaf 'Angel' pelargonium, it has small pretty leaves, offset with flowers of pale mauve with maroon blotches. Plants will

thrive best in brightly lit, slightly sheltered conditions, where the colouration of the leaves will become rich and glowing.
'Scarlet Unique' This cultivar has much smaller flowers than 'Crimson Unique', but grows into a larger, and more lax, spreading shrub which will have an eventual height of almost 60cm (24in). The flowers are very showy scarlet with darker dot-markings. 'Scarlet Unique' is a good choice for growing in any mixed summer planting, creating an informal, colourful display.
'Seeley's Pansy' A modern American variety which has lax growth and small, dark leaves. The flowers are small, white with a purple blotch on each of the upper petals and are produced throughout the summer. Grown for a couple of years in a hanging basket or pot, this variety will create a stunning and most unusual display in any garden.
'Sefton' An award-winning 'Regal' cultivar which was introduced in 1994. The flowers are cerise-red, the petals blazed and feathered with deeper red, arranged in large clusters. Plants will grow to about 40cm (16in) tall and are wonderful grown in specimen pots as a focal point in a prominent location.

'The Boar' A most unusual, single-flowered, 'Zonal' cultivar which has lax, trailing stems to 60cm (24in) long. The leaves are mid-green, with

'Mrs Pollock'

a dark purple-black centre. The salmon-pink flowers are produced freely throughout the growing season.
'Voodoo' Introduced in 1972, this impressive 'Unique' cultivar grows to a robust 60cm (24in) tall. The leaves are triangular rather than lobed, and are a good foil to the velvety burgundy flowers with a purple-black throat. A lovely plant for a container.
'Wendy Read' Probably produced in the early 1970s, this popular cultivar comes into flower early in the season. The leaves are softly zoned with a dark band, and act as a good foil to the double, salmon-pink flowers, which shade out to almost white. They make a strong statement.

Index

ACKNOWLEDGEMENTS
The author and publisher would
like to thank: Hazel Ann Flowers,
Quarry Cottages, Wall Hill Road,
Ashurstwood, Sussex RH19 3TQ;
Orchard Nursery, Holtye Road,
East Grinstead, West Sussex
RH19 3PP; Jardinerie, Evesham
Road, Cheltenham, Gloucestershire;
Yoma Bock, Coton Manor Garden,
Nr. Guilsborough, Northamptonshire,
NN6 8RQ; Fibrex Nurseries,
Honeybourne Road, Pebworth,
Stratford-upon-Avon CV37 8XT;
Mr and Mrs Harrison. The
photographs on pages 14 and 64
(bottom left) are courtesy of Peter
Anderson. The photographs on pages
56–7 are courtesy of Peter McHoy.